Poetry of a female Painter

Poetry from the silk artist Stefanie Wilhelm

Von Stefanie Wilhelm

S.Wilhelm
Stralsunder Str.2
19063 Schwerin, MV

Telefon: +491629790846
Stefaniasilkarts@gmail.com

Poetry of a female Painter

Stefanie Wilhelm

Das Buch:

Inspired by Pablo Nehruda's "Twenty Love Poems and a Song of Despair" I thought, that twenty Poems for an unpublished poet is just the right size! And so I chose 20 poems that would more or less describe some of the most emotional chapters of my life so far.

Equipped with a lot of imagination from childhood on, her first poem was initially secretly written about a certain hotel guest, behind the counter of a four-star hotel, during the time she worked as a receptionist.

Der Autor:

"My love is my art is my home"

Stefanie Wilhelm writes poetry to turn her restless thoughts into some kind of beauty, adding spice and reason to her existence. As an active Silkpainter named Stefaniasilkarts, she finally committed herself to sending her poetry into space. Welcome to her art, which she shares with followers and international artists. She worked in Germany, England, and Austria, with longer stays in Greece, Costa Rica, and Spain. Her desire to travel remains untamed.

Poetry of a female Painter

Prosa

von

Stefanie Wilhelm

Amazon Self-publishing

1. Edition, 2024

S.Wilhelm

Stralsunder Str.2

19063 Schwerin, MV

Stefaniasilkarts@gmail.com

Inhaltsverzeichnis

la instantanea No°11   76

la Instantánea No°6 76

Loyalties

Please know that I am tremendously grateful for your interest in my thoughts and the poetry that escaped my mind, of which you hold a copy in your hands. You touch me, quite literally. This is my first self-published book about poetry, and to all readers (in case of audio, listeners) please also note: I wish to encourage all writers, artists, poets, thinkers, and people who think and dream of having their own written book in your hands but could not yet overcome the hurdles, circumstances, resistance that is standing in your way:

Jump!

Stop those endless moments of over thinking,

stop hesitating and just *run*.

All else will follow

Remember: You have to believe to make it happen.

Let's make this beautiful miracle now.

GATE TO PARADISE

Sweetly
you talk of Paradise.
There's a garden door, an open gate,
wondrous ways that lead us
into a universe, full of hidden treasures.
Promises.
Your wisdom, infinitely
so beautifully shared,
in clear blue vision.

Magical ways that bewitch us
with a chart of colours that are voluptuous.
Flashing fierce reds that are fighting
against the cooling green of shadows.
Emerald greens, violent blues,
bright shimmering turquoise.

Only to be interrupted
from sudden calming
golden rays of light.
There's a unity
of wilderness, of sea sife, of birds.

Busy with themselves.
Unintimidated by human kind,
as if to say: "Who are you"?
From this refuge, this
fragile land of plenty, of wonders
In this whole universe of urgency, of nature
we have only
but one heart to set on fire,
we have only
but one heart to give.

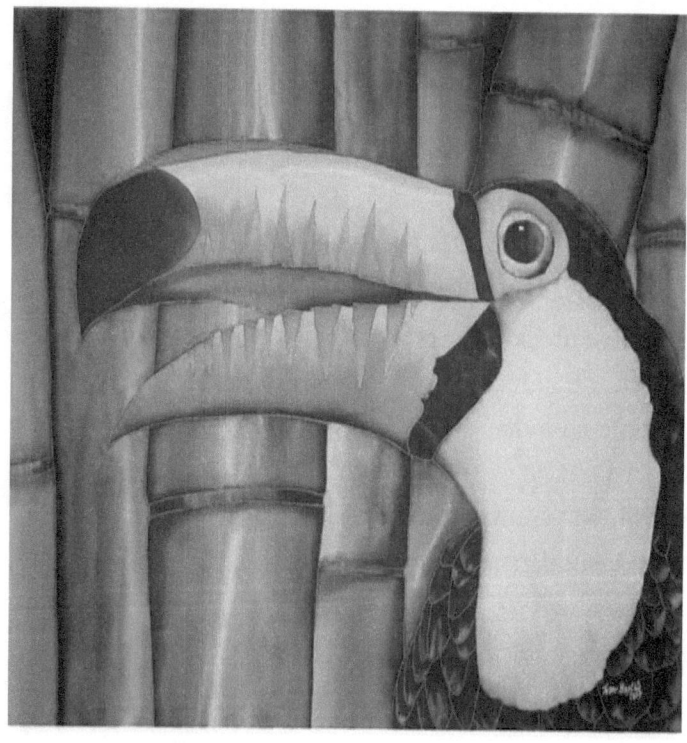

This lovely Toco-Toucan has all Copyrights with its Creator, Daniel Jean-Baptist, Master silk painter, Saint Lucia / Canada.

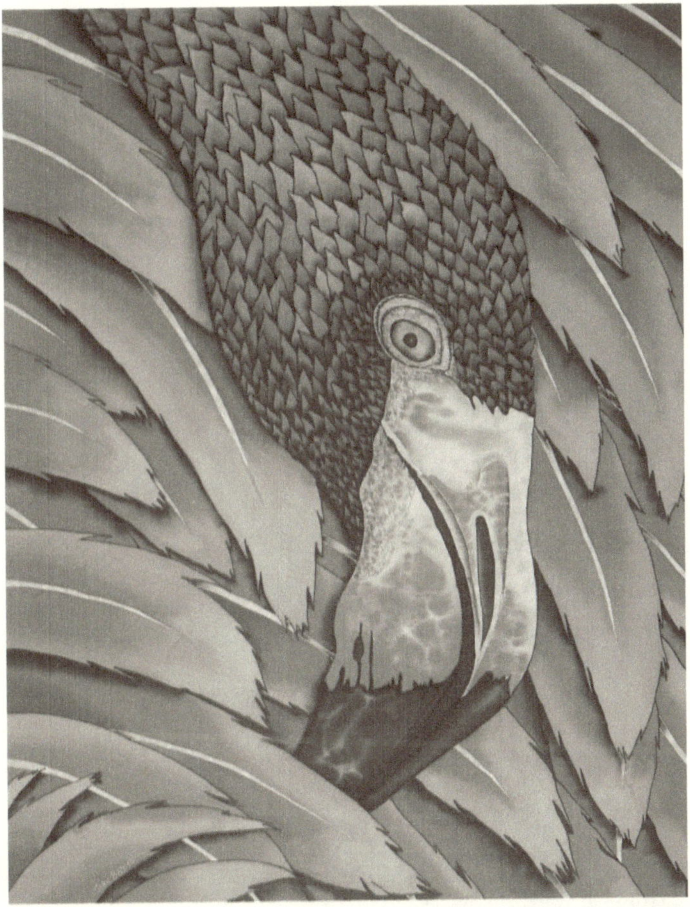

![toucan silk painting]

Silkart / Copyright Daniel Jean-Baptiste.
https://www.jean-baptiste.com

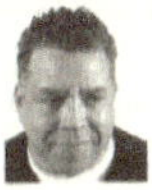

FEELING GROOVY

Slightly used n'groovy
I like your style.
A bit of bondage, too -
you know how to tease.

We are in tune, together
have a great alliance
when we start to dance
sometimes bold and swift
we do so
wholeheartedly
without fear or doubts
and love to dip in deep, although
some happy accidents may occur.
Always ready for it. Still
your touch so gently and light when needed
precise up to the point
I know you can hold it
(have never let me down so far).

And yet you are a tough one
you express my feelings

with you I travel
some beautiful uncovered avenues
Of shape, of colour, of heart and truth.
I could not do without your presence
and when I am holding you in my hands...
its happy hour without closing time.
Your my companion
a dear friend
and my most beloved
Hairy paint brush.

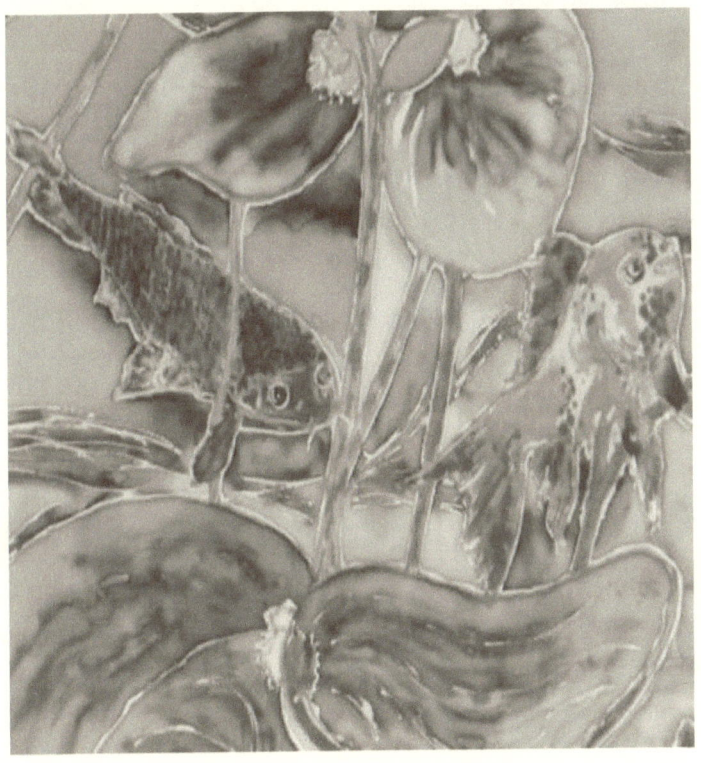

Stefanie Wilhelm

THE FLOW

I woke up one day
to find you.
Oh, you blew me
the first time I caught sight
you were taking me by full surprise.

No fear of heights.

I have
no safety net or guiding lines
with you
it's all
FREEFALL
a wet embrace
eternal flowing river.
You ask me to follow
upon your siren song,
swirling beauty
your fire within me.

When I surrender,
I am lost for words.
Yet what are words?
Red is a word,
Passion is a word.
Death and rebirth, love are words too.
Without you, my silk would feel lonely.

Unsure of the challenge in your offering
you give nothing but full-heartedly:
in raging tender embrace
joyous sparks of colour
that gracefully dive
into divine profoundness
the spirit of infinite creation.

Hooked
to your irresistible,
seductive charms.
I can trust your true blue.

A simple journey
where my silk is my canvas
a canopy of velvet Stars.
Perhaps a dream of Butterflies
or Fishes, singing in the night.

Stefanie Wilhelm

BEACHED BOAT

I have found a treasure.
A beached boat.
Stranded. Lonely, calm.

What is its story?
Why has it been abandoned?
The scene so peaceful and tender.

No storm in sight,
although a broken mast.
A kiss... of soft and folly winds
that are playing with the sails,
simple moods of a lazy day.
A mere tease,
memories of better days.
Waves which cheerfully embraced the boats timber
gently rocking it sideways.

The boat has a leek, a puddle inside its belly.
The rocks give shelter, provide company.
Perhaps a long wait
in your beached fortress,
confinement of forgotten pleasures.
An ancient heart, yearning for the currents.
Still, she is beautiful, fearless and full of vigor.

Meanwhile...

The boat, waiting in sleepy bewilderment
has met its Waterloo.

My dear,
I cannot solve the riddle.
Was it a young boy who secretly went fishing?
Has he forgotten the boat?
Where they lovers, running away
from a home in a rush?
Did you go to the market?

Looking at this painting
I feel the open wound.
I am touching both:
Past and Eternity -
Stars the shiver in the sea at night,
the offering of unease.

Despite there is a happy valley
Transient, rich, volatile.
Full splendor of a grand midsummer's day.

Decay faraway
and wonderful its being,
the absence of lament.

Nicky is charming, and his smart advises as an Artist
helped me to free my mind of others' input hence to
kick start my inner child running a little looser. I am
grateful he showed me his art that day,
when the beauty of his soul certainly spoke to mine.

Stefanie Wilhelm

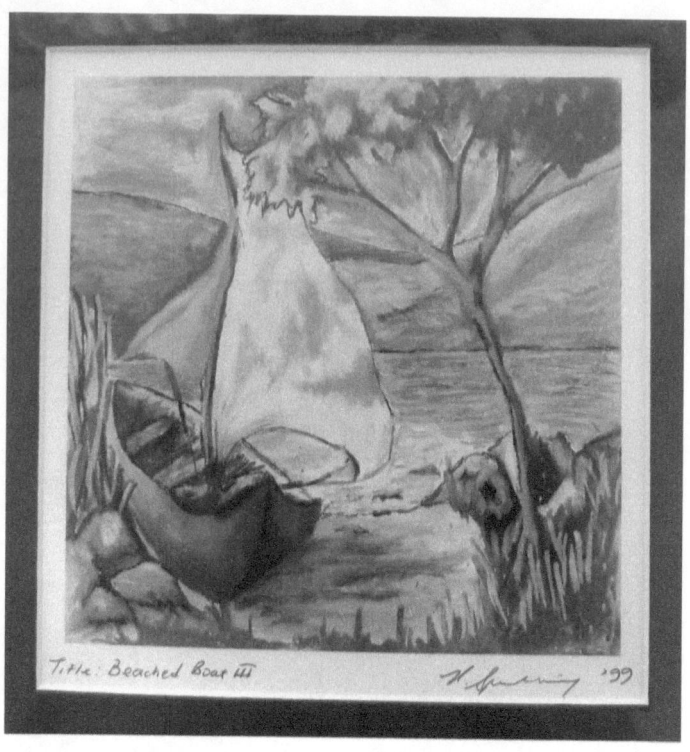

Gouache painting "Beached Boat" Copyrights with
Nicky Spaulding Arts, Miami

This lovely gouache painting "Beached Boat" has been
presented to me after my visit to Nicky's Art Studio in
Miami.
Unforgettable the afternoon in this hot humid month of
July, this is a splendid reminder!

HEART IN WINTER

I love the icy rain.
Then, you cannot see the tears
running over my face.
Furious winds blowing, teasing
my heart in winter.

Somewhere, deep in the hidden south
must still be heard a songbird singing.
I am searching for spells to break the chain.

More than a hundred
perhaps if only one could be sufficient?
While you, with your tiger stone eyes
still circling above me like an Eagle
still hunting in the Garden of Eden
believing your way.

In my hands:
The formidable sword of a Gladiator
dauntless and strong.

High upon the sheltered grassland
I am waiting for you.
Covered by a roof of stars, embracing the night
yearning for your tenderness. Oh, I miss
your warming body
and in my dream, sleeping

until dawn wakes us joyfully
leaving the darkness behind us.

Strengthened and fresh
we will shake away the shadows
and start
a brand-new day.

VULCANO IN LOVE WITH THE AEGEAN SEA

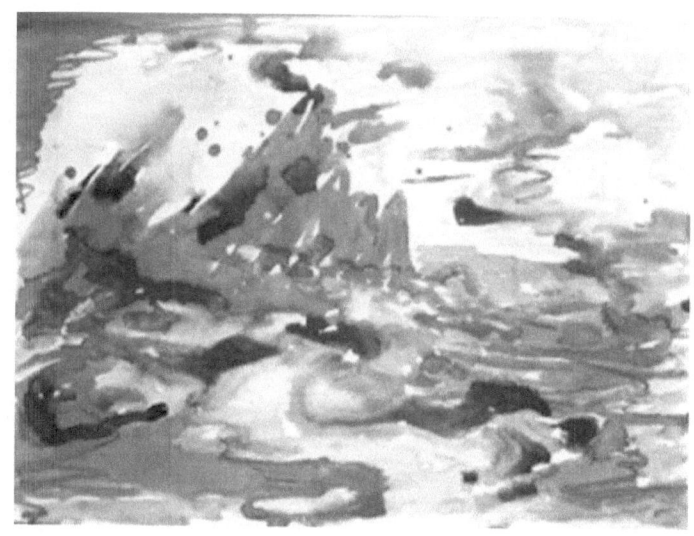

Dedicated to Greece and its People.
Gouache, Copyright: Stefanie Wilhelm

SIXTY SECOND'S POETRY

Imagine poetry for everyone. So short and sweet, if you
do not like poetry you can still enjoy some that have the
power to reach your heart for a brief moment only.
Sixty seconds only.
Perhaps even a little less time. For beauty.
That much, everyone can handle.
Even in our fast-living times, between your scroll on
Instagram.
Sixty seconds that can make or break your day, can make
you smile, can take you to a new dimension.
Since they come and go in an instant,
I teasingly call them

'la instantanea'

and they have numbers, too.
You will come across them from time to time,
happily arranged quite by accident.

Stefanie Wilhelm

TARA BODDHISATVA

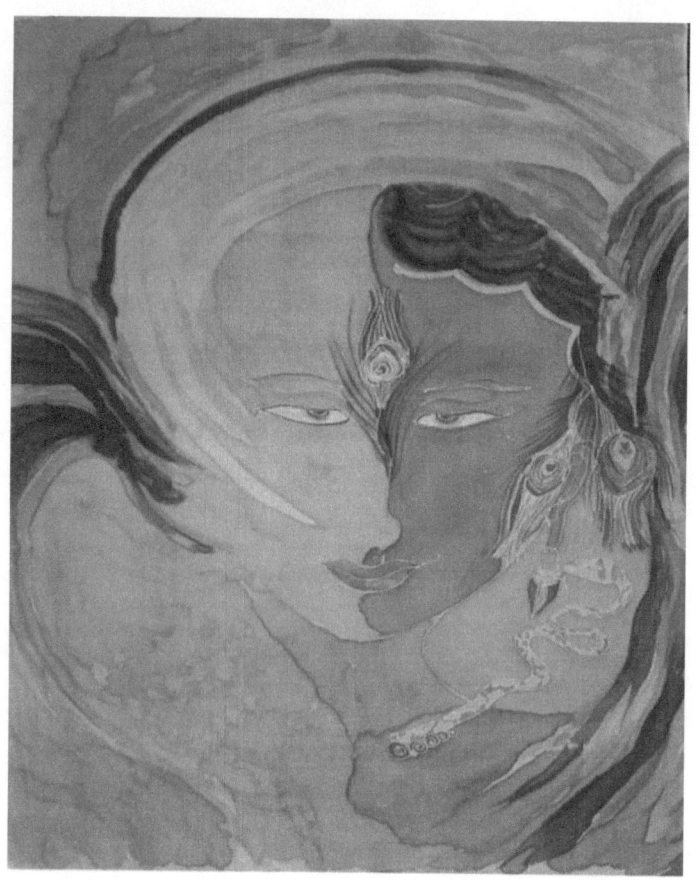

This is the lovely TARA (as I called her) Boddhisatva, Mother of Buddha, originally the daughter of an Indian Goddess of Stars. Tara is kind and peaceful, born out of tears of empathy.

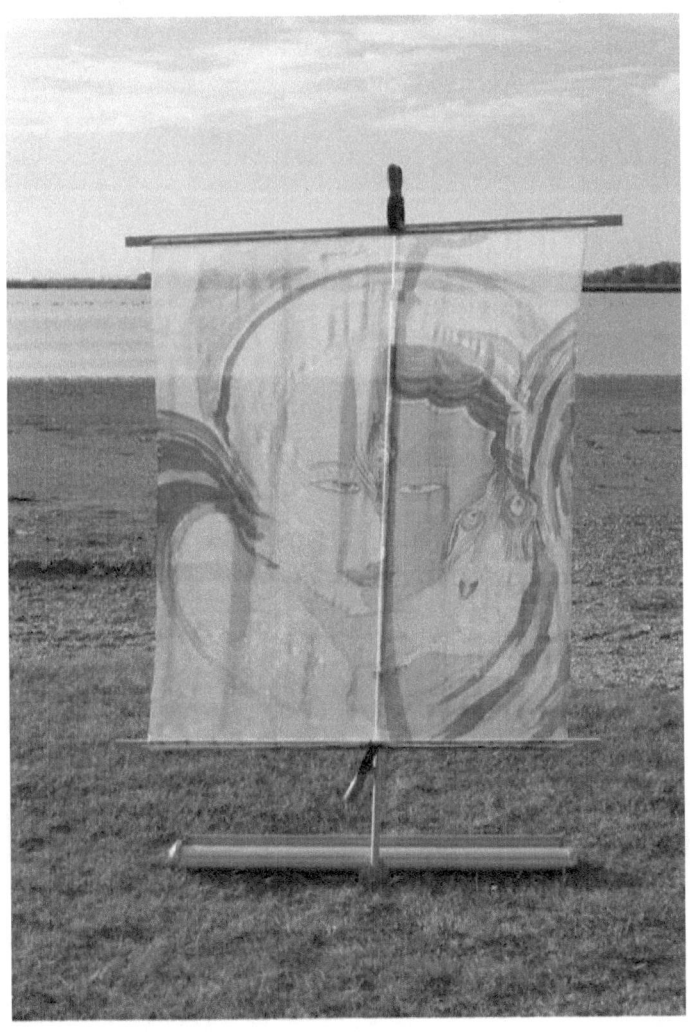

In my version, she turned half into an Angel, when she was hearing my friend, Maria singing live during our first performance together.

Watch this Video here:
(Maria Lapteva & Stefaniasilkarts : Arien, Romantische Operette und Malerei auf Seide) Our first live evening together in Austria at SKA Klinik Zicksee.

https://www.youtube.com/watch?v=LJ020wbPNN0&t=2273

la instantánea No°4

Nothing can harm me.

*

Not even you.

SHE'S GOT THE BLUES

Some are waiting for my lines of poetry.

Forgive to see their essence:
Vinegar.
Drops of acid
on white clean sheets.
Each
to burn my heart
in simple lines
of written excuses.

I daresay I wonder
what is it all about.

Ha!
There is
no sunshine, no romance
no moonlight serenades.
HOW ON EARTH
shall I write a poem?
It is Sunday, my dear.
(As if that says it all)

The blues
crept into my shivering cells
that are still alive
but thirsty.

You see, I have no defense
against my own shadows.

If I stare at myself in the mirror
I see those wide opened eyes
that provide not even a single answer.

I would wish to transform
into a poppy flower, melting
in fields of Himalayan blue, of pinks and
red-orange that can move with the wind
unsheltered and free.

We would build an army of happiness,
soldiers of light
that are chatting with butterflies
and give standing ovation
in awe of their beauty.

Those sucking blood lice
irritating as ever
could finally go and hide
in their closets.

la instantánea No°7

**It is not love that I fear.
It is falling in love,**

where the trouble is hiding.

A MATTER OF SWEETNESS

The smart people tell you:
"One has to be smart in live"
('Cause if you act dumb, you lose out)

The logical people tell you:
"One has to be organized"
(Otherwise, you will end up in chaos)

The rich people tell you:
"It is all about Money, you have got to make Money!
(Without it you are buggered up)

Then comes someone, who whispers softly:
"Sweet is the best part of living" ...

la instantánea No°6

Heroes!

Love to be:
A H.e.r.o.

Honest
Excited
Real
Optimistic.

Quite Extraordinary.
It is a little sexy, don't you think?

It really
does not need that much
to be a hero.

It takes it all!

Just be.
A Hero.
For me.

Heroes II

Throughout the years of history:
Your history, our story.
Look at
those fields, those
empty forgotten graves.
Rotten Shipwrecks, long forgotten.
They have been dying for years,
so long ago.
Once
they have all been Heroes.
Although there is no glory
in shining armor,
there is no glory in war.
Still, we all need Heroes.

Heroes that shine, outshine
unworthy glimmering City Lights
that blind you in false pretends.
Peaceful Warriors
that fight another kind of holy war.

Some fight a war of Mango trees,
strange wars that nobody knows of,
with brushes in their hand,
in a land of fantasy
while others do so with tint and a feather:
They fight in words of poetry,

with love and kindness:
Spiritual Souls
which simply live their lives as Gladiators.

When you talk to me,
you speak softly – so I may hear you.
When you act – you act boldly
so I may follow.
You can come too:
We meet at the cornerstone,
the one
that is easy to find:

Just rise above yourself
search inside your heart
and when you sing,

you sing a song of joy.

la instantánea No°10

**I am hungry.
My favorite color of today
would be**

chocolate.

THE SOUND OF DRUMS

You can hear them, they are
following the call of their ancient companions:
There, on the side of the road,
not far away from us
Did you too saw
those tread down hearts,
their last drink
some lost streamlets of blood
heavily united, running
as a rushing river.

May their wishes come to be true,
blue true.
May the power and desire
surge
like a leaf that dances
above the southern sea.
Full of beauty and fantasy
breaking their swords
still
silently smiling
while spinning in their orbits.

This Poem I was writing in awe of those ancient and
modern   Aztecs and Mexicans that fighting for their
existence, dying.
In the Mountains of Mexico, February 1991
Dieses   Gedicht   widme   ich   allen   Azteken   und
Mexikanern, die in diesen Tagen, kämpfend um Ihre
Existenz, in den Bergen Mexikos ausgelöscht werden -
Februar 1991

Trommellaute

Durch den Weg der Geschichte
folgen Sie dem Ruf alter Gefährten:
Auf dem Wegesrand,
nicht weit entfernt von uns:
Zertretene Herzen,
kannst du Sie sehen?
Ihr letzter Trank
entfliesst wie ein Rinnsaal
der sich wieder findet,
blutig vereinigt
zum rauschenden Fluss.

Mögen Eure Wünsche Wahrheit werden,
möge die Kraft und Sehnsucht
sich wiegen wie ein Blatt im Meer.
Gefüllt der Schönheit und Fantasie

Ihrer Schwerter brechend
dochlautlos lächelnd Ihrer Bahnen bewusst.

Statue of the Dancer Conchero Chichimeca, historic
town Santiago de Queretaro, UNESCO World Heritage
Site, Province of Queretaro, Mexico, Central America.

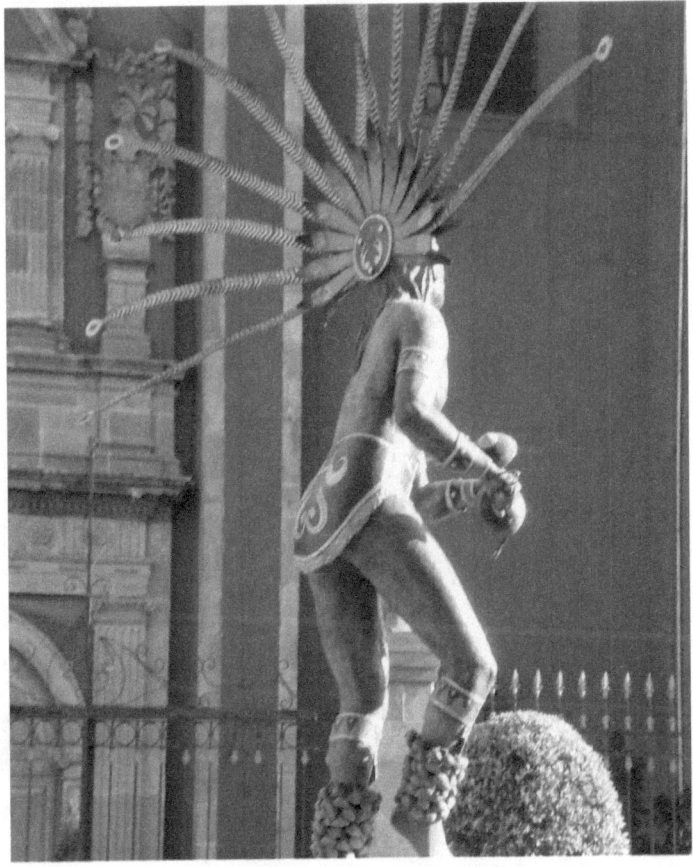

(This foto was taken by myself in Ciudad Santiago de
Queretaro, Mx, in March 2012)

Stefanie Wilhelm

Xokonoschtletl Gómora

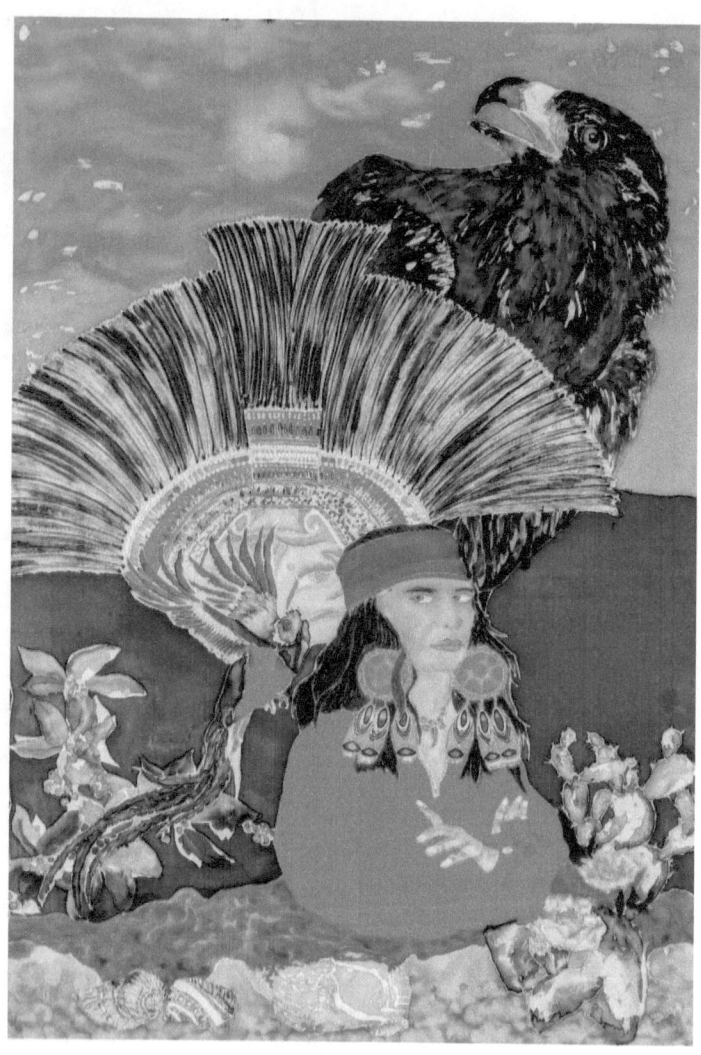

I painted this silk painting of the Aztec Dancer, Drummer, Author, UN-Speaker
Xokonoschtletl Gómora for a fine reason:

Together we have an association in Vienna and I support his mission, the return of the sacred Feathercrown from the 9th Montezuma King back to Mexico.
She is 500 Years in Exile and Xokonoschtletl fights over 40 years for her return.
You can support his mission, please.
We further fight vividly to urgently save some 8 HA of rainforest close to his home in Tabasco, Mx.
This area will be cleared for use of cattle.
We want to secure it and keep its precious wildlife save!
In the south of Mexico in the state of Tabasco, 8 hectares of tropical rainforest have recently been cleared!
Cattle are to graze there in future, as they need open spaces and, above all, grass. At least 150 old trees will be felled for this!

This land lies in the middle of the ancient Mayan territory, and their buildings can still be found in the immediate vicinity. The world-famous Palenque is also not far away! It is now home to countless plants, trees and animals. There are mahogany trees, mandarin, papaya and mango trees, howler and spider monkeys, anteaters, eagle owls, wild boars, turtles, iguanas, parrots, zebra herons, butterflies and many others... A river about 70 meters wide runs through the property, in which the well-known manatees and fish of various species weighing up to 8 kg can be found!

The indigenous people fish there and feed on what nature gives them; this river has its source in the Usumacinta, which is considered sacred in Mexico and flows into nearby Guatemala.

Tabasco is the gateway to the Mayan world and also the land of the Olmecs, the oldest Mexican civilization. Bananas, cocoa and chewing gum trees still grow here, and 53% of the world's water resources are found in Tabasco. It has 1,640 lagoons and is only 8 meters above sea level! The average temperature is 27 degrees.

Please help us to save this land and protect it from destruction! Every little amount helps! All donors will receive a real feather from Mexico as a small thank you! Please send us your address in return.

We are talking about a total area of 8 hectares, we have to buy at least 4 hectares! The price per hectare is € 3,800. For comparison: in Germany you would have to reckon with € 13,000 to € 60,000 per hectare of forest - without the river...

Attention: Your donation is very urgent!

The owner doesn't give us much time!

Please share this campaign with your friends, acquaintances, family, colleagues, on Facebook, Instagram etc.
Please don't forget: every little amount is needed!
Our fundrasing campagnes are here:

https://gofund.me/0ca756d5

https://gofund.me/cee7ffd7

More Info on Xokonoschtletl is to be found at the end of my book. Thank you for your kind understanding.

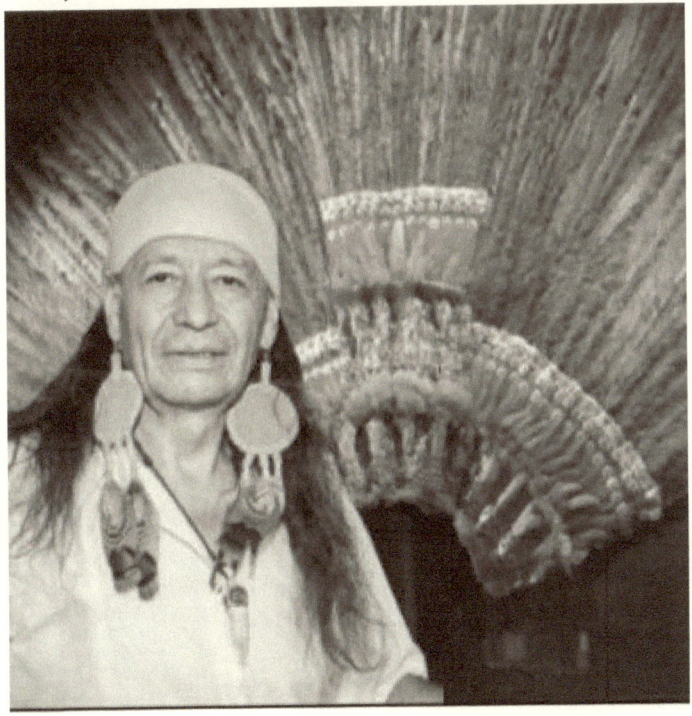

Stefanie Wilhelm

TATTOO

I cannot describe you

the Loneliness

that has captured my heart,
like a huge blue moon
causing me
this total eclipse.
Neither
can I describe you
how I have made it,
up to now,
day by day – surviving.

So far, supposedly
I am doing fine
with my lasting torments
understanding
for the first time
the true meaning
of patience, knowing:
there is nothing
to hurry anymore.
There is no need for anger
because I have lost you
and, reassuringly
that I still love you.

Mi Corazon:

The marks that we have left
each other:
Nobody can see them.

Only you and I
know of their existence.
Only you and I
can understand
their great pain, their great comfort.
They are like laser prints,
burnt deeply
into our heart and soul.

They have torn us to pieces, yet
it is precisely "because"
that we will not forget each other.
So should you
if even just once,
in one single nano moment
of that eternal life of yours
(which we all share)
may think, may believe
that we do not belong,
Let me tell you:
You are mistaken.

You must know:
This Tattoo of ours
is consisting

of a string of DNA
with two sides – one
for each of us.

Even in the greatest
of universal mass material,
we would recognize each other,
there is no denial.
In my loneliness
this shall be my comfort.

Whether it might be
in the darkest of darkness
the furthest from far;
In the brightest of Sun and Stars:
I will find you again, always.
Lately, you chose to be
"The sunshine of my life"
with that, I have to be content
at least, for a while,
to live my life among this Earth.

When we, my love
are finally to meet each other again,
soul to soul
in our spiritual ways:
We will feel only
forgiveness and eternal youth.
Our smiles, rays of light
will be as one.

There will be nothing left

from past furies, desperation,
sadness, struggle.
Only then, my best one,
will we have made it, together.
Arriving
at that holy grail, bathing
in its healing touch.
Our haunted hearts:
Mutually, calm, untied.
Our happiness,
forever loving, peacefully
will be the essence
of time
and laughter.

Stefanie Wilhelm

la instantánea No°9

Let us kiss and turn to stone,
in eternity
in that mutual feeling
of fun and love.

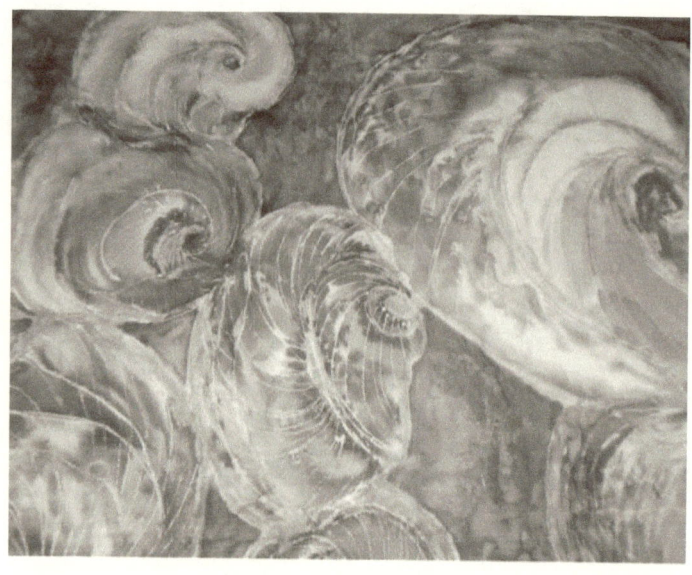

„Caramello Seashells" by Stefaniasilkarts

YOU WILL NOT FIND ME

You will not find me
waiting in line.

I will always be the one
standing outside the crowd.
You will not find me among those
eagerly chasing you
I am the one
to watch over your shadow.

If you want to find me
do not search far.
Look for me
in a faraway land
where we can hide our love
under the shadow of the fig tree leaves
away
from the eyes of a jealous sky.

When the Songbird sings
so gracefully
I will be standing close.

This is the time
for travelers of hearts
of minds
we tie our hearts together

with tiny delicate knots
where the blue moon shines
over fragrant waters
on fired tender beaches
throwing our fisher's net
into that sea of love
sharing the gift
that we bring to each other.

Lost in eternal kisses
our kisses will be mutual
since love is a battle of light
it dances
as the swallows do
in their circling of skies
as the dolphins do
in waves of unity
of mutual delight.

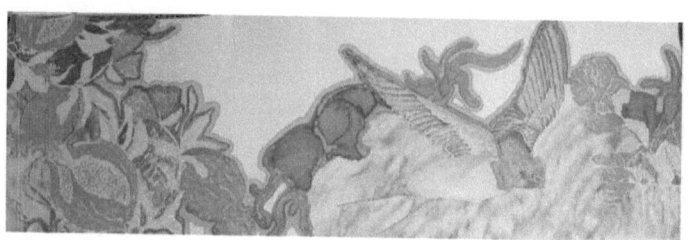

„Spring Awakening"
Copyright Stefaniasilkarts

WE ARE ARTISTS

Not
because we are more educated,
more talented, or anything better
neither would we even understand more of art
than others, No.

We are Artists
because we stronger connect
with the sensualities,
with our natural yearning for freedom in us
and no longer can we bear to subdue
that wanting.

It is this wish, the haunting longing
and contention within ourselves
which takes us closer
to the experience of our own creativity.

Therefore
there is no other way for us
except to live, to search, go deeper,
follow and explore
along those longitudes
and express our inner siren
trying to find an answer in art.

OCEAN BLUE

Still the Ocean is blue.
My blue, blue of the deep sea.
Song of blue.

Deep fulfilling blue
so deep, it is inhaling you,
wanting
to become one with you.
Ocean waters. Motion in blue.

Elixir of life
of soul, of prism
of clarity, of emotion.
Tender rays of light that dance
to caress us
in space an isolation.

I stand at the shore
inhaling the sea
in its noble turquoise lavishness.
Watching inquisitive waves
that come to talk,
tempting me, teasing
with their salty spice.

You can feel the wind
hear the seagull's cry

while they kiss
with their wings
the foam of sea breeze.
Not far away
cheerful and bright
some white merry sails
sailing along, crossing
through a mere happy summers' day.

Someone
is waving at me.

I join into their sunny moods
gazing at the edge of infinity
conscious
that what I know of
is insignificant.

In case the winds will change
with folly clouds that lift me
as they do with a feather
to travel along those longitudes
as my fingers do
in lonely nights.
I will be ready
for your arms to take me,
we would emerge in fires,
in light
that nothing can extinguish
but an ocean of love.

la instantánea No°2

**Just in case! I am keeping my sails
wide open.
Ready for the wind
to melt with my wings,
It's getting me out of the doldrums**

AN AFTER WORK-PARTY

We met and were both without Umbrellas.
It was raining heavily and unpleasantly cool,
Gale winds blowing too.
Huriedly we were looking for a cosy place that would
shelter us, and we found rescue at our spectacular
Church in Town today. Sitting there for some
two-and-a-half hours.
Despite there being no heating...
Except that we were reading Poetry.

And Erotic Stories.

LUMIÈRE DE LA NUIT

I wrote this poem in Frankfurt when I was transiently a licensed taxi-driver. Imagine an icy cold winter night, glittering streets, snow just stopped falling.
It was January, around two o'clock in the early morning. Just a few late-night party owls around, here or there, passing by.
There I was, waiting in line, along with a few more taxis for a possible stranger in need for a drive home.
The city lights were all but cold blue while the Bronze Statue of Bull and Bear, standing in front of Frankfurt's old Stock Exchange, started to flirt with my mind.

Frankfurt, Börsenplatz:

Ein Stier widersteht dem Winter:
Kalt glitzert die Straße im Vollmondlicht.
Noch
ist der junge Schnee weiß,
spiegeln Eiskristalle auf deinem Bronzerücken
blauschimmerndes Stadtlicht wieder.
Noch
brennen Striemen auf meiner Haut,

Zeugnis meiner Sehnsucht.
Gebrauche mich, zügele mich
so benutze ich dich, verzehre mich
an Dir.

Einsam und verlassen die Straßen.
Ich lehne mich
an deine frostigen Schultern.
Kühle mich.
Der warme Atem deiner Nüstern
umgibt mich,
erotisiert mich.
Süße Intoxikation meiner Sinne.

Ich erwache von neuem
wie eine Wüstenrose im Morgentau.
Spät erst, früh am Morgen
löse ich mich von Dir.
Wir werden uns wiedersehen,
werden uns erneut
aneinander gewöhnen,
aneinander reiben
vertiefen die Spuren
nicht alltäglicher Nächte;

Werden wir
nach und nach

unsere Unschuld verlieren,

beglücken uns

im Lumière unserer Leidenschaft.

la instantánea No°1

It is high time
for love
to be
reinvented.

Stefanie Wilhelm

LEMON DANCE

Tender the night in early autumn.

A City in dreams.
Dreams
of rich summer moments
of an old-fashioned dance
that is spiced
by the sweet and vigorous ways
of lemon fall.

A snail escaped
the torment of time.
Time which never cares.
People. Lost for love,
their innocent journey
in a life full of longing.
Beggars or Knights
in a Kingdom of Hearts.

You and me

distantly we share
the same nostalgia
the same fragile hopes.
So beautifully impossible
for a stolen kiss
such daring Expectations!

Behind the cat...
Someone is watching in secret:
So to give birth
to a paradise in waiting,
in wisdom
maybe
singing a little song.

Quietly
for himself and the Moon
just loud enough
not to disturb
the nights solitude,
its beauty
and its peaceful
bygone lament.

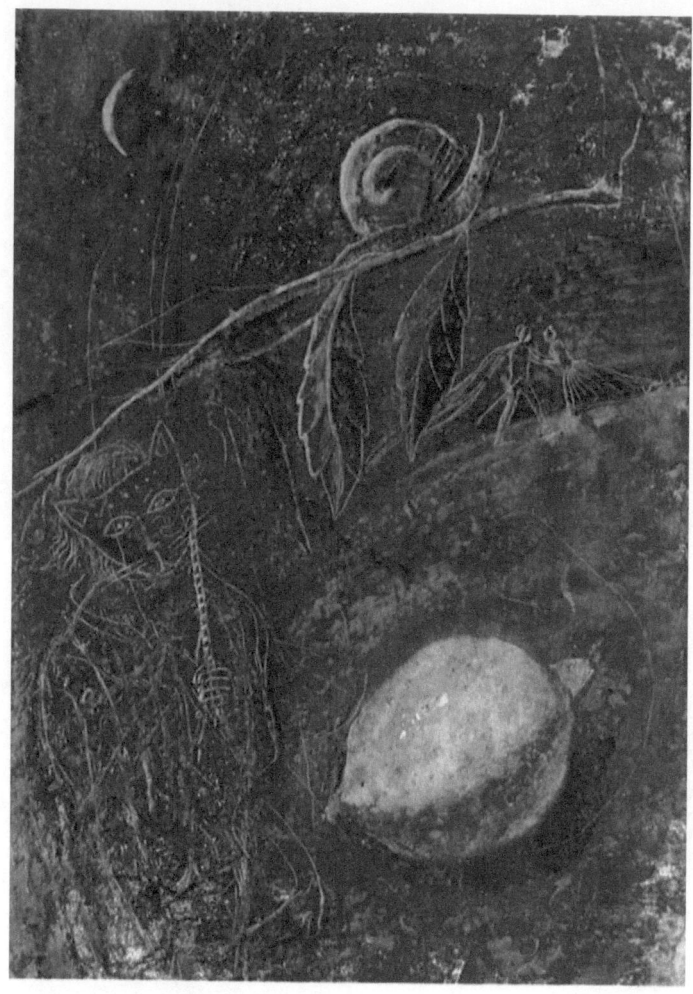

This beautiful Artwork was created with Oil crayons from Mahmud Mahmudzade, Baku, AZ Mahmud's wonderful art has led me to create my poem "Lemon dance". Thank you, my dear friend.
It was given to me afterwards as a beautiful present.

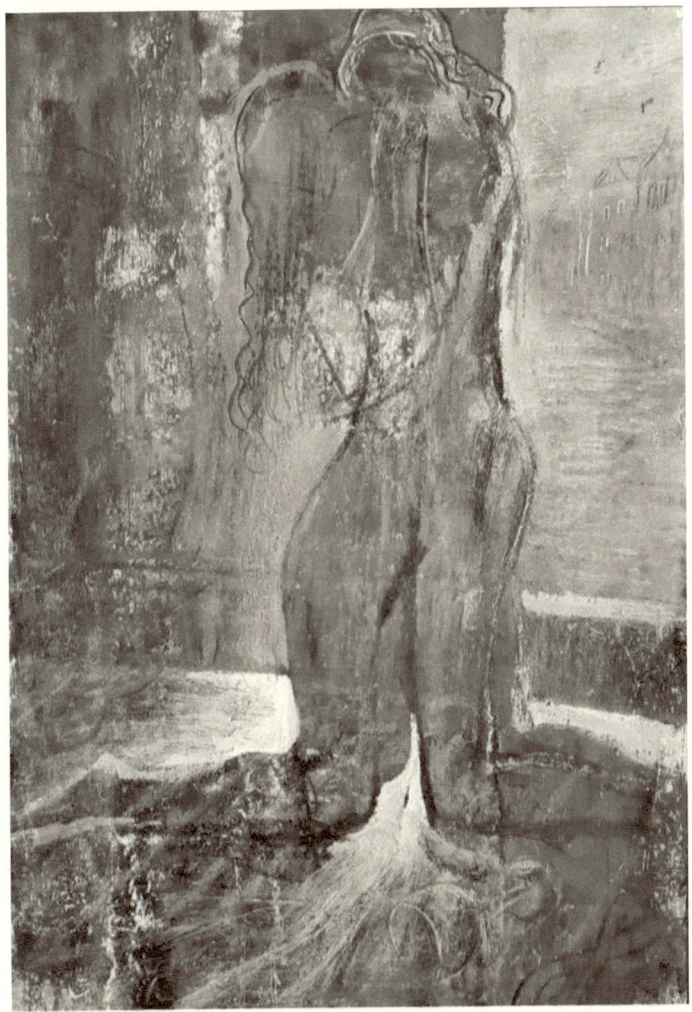

https://www.facebook.com/ccorona64
It is such a joy and pleasure for me to have friends who can create art such as these two lovers.
Copyright Mahmud Mahmudzade.

la instantánea No°3

I'd love to sleep

in the Palm

of your hands.

Thoughts on silk painting

Clearly: I am not a precision painter.
I suspect that even with lots of practice... I might never become one. Although I adore it.
Because it is not my nature, sometimes in the flow of colors, emotions... I get carried away with my creative work, even though ... I do take notice on detail. And I realize: I am simply not a perfectionist. I just do not seem to have the capacity for it, my temper sings a different mode, performs to a different tune.
So I have to show great patience with myself, reminding me over again to take more time, if I am not to ruin my beloved pieces of Silk while working on a new creation.

The beauty of Silk painting is this:
It allows you to perform to many different styles. You just have to find your way. There are great, wonderful painters that work in precision style, with excellence to each point or stroke of their brush. (Years of practice and devotion!)
And there are others who paint in wonderful freestyle, creating full flow motion paintings.

I am somewhere in-between with a great tendency towards abstract painting.
Since I am more and more accepting, embracing this reality and literally go with my flow (of colors, of shape) and do not be too concerned by the "correctness" of my paintings... They become deeper, better and have a stronger message.
And I love it.

la instantánea No.5

**Selling Art
is
an Art.**

Stefanie Wilhelm

RAIN ON RHODES

They warn me of the rain.
Rain on Rhodes.
If it rains here, it rains.

The air is heavy with this rain.
Since days.
She is like a heavily pregnant woman.
First, the sun disappears.
Then the clouds move in.
Slow clouds, that hover
and do not move away.

I can smell this rain, too.
Rain that does not show itself
or would simply poor down
like a Caribbean rain – No.
This rain has a waiting list!

There is thunder in the air
while the wind
that slashes the leaves against my window
in the night,
that same wind
howls over the sea
which turns dark green and grey
wearing a crown of short, bity waves

becoming one with those clouds.

They dampen, thicken themselves
lay moist and heavy on your mind.
Cooling you down
your skin
cooling those walls
your linen, there is no escape
from this rain,
which still
does not appear.

In the morning, finally
the rain is raining, it drains.
My tree outside the window
is crying heavily.
Big tears running down
its tree leaves
they build whole avenues
running back
into the Aegean Sea.

And as the cats
those shy Island cats
of Rhodes do,
that now
have all but disappeared
into their hiding places,
their street palaces -
Much the same, I wish to take shelter
in my pillows, if only
to wait it out.

Only my alarm clock
reminds me, knocks me out
"There is no space for
such trivial pursuit".
Never mind the rain
there still is business as usual,
and no umbrella in my suitcase.

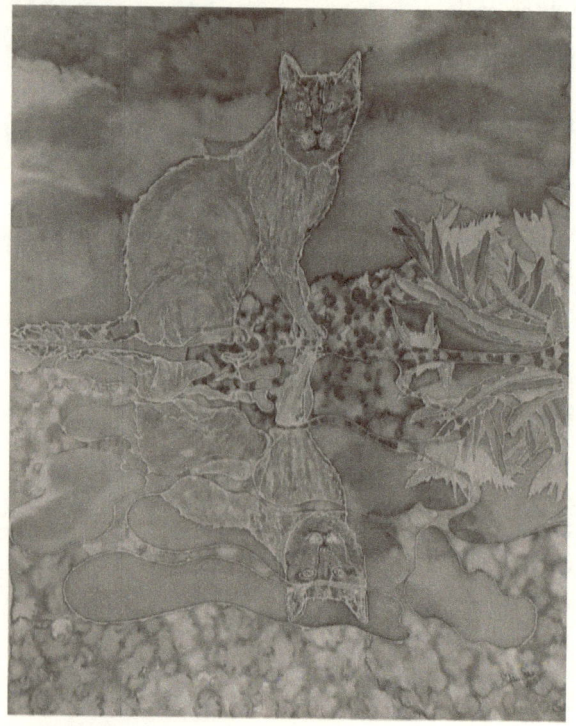

"Harbour cat" Silkart by Stefaniasilkarts.
A shy city harbor cat of Rhodes, a rover that waits for
the sun to reappear. Do you think, he has a name?

la instantánea No°24

I cannot have my sun.
So I have asked for a lighthouse.

Instead, I received a firefly.

Clearly my angel has a wicked sense of humour.

la instantánea No°15

The art of erotic
is inbetween.

SILVERMOON

I see myself
pending, howling like a Wolf
at my Silvermoon.
Yet I am no Wolf.
I am of Morphus.
Morphus Blue, Morpho Peleides
Corpus of transition
Corpus of desire.

My Soul
wants to be free.
Of itself,
away from you,
away from me.
Meanwhile
I am drawn, hypnotized
in painful wanting.

Silencio. Another silent Night.
I am bathing

in your radiation.
Your silver shines
touches my skin, cooling me
with a feathered breeze.

There are no mortal sins
that escape my being.
Just you and me.
Every so often
gravitated from your pulling powers
I am losing a scale.
They dance around me
in swirling reflections
that I cannot follow
'cause you trill me
with that tidal hold.
From time to time
I am released
by Daybreak.

Then, once again
I become
just a simple butterfly.
Flutter off into the winds
entirely to embrace the sun
entirely to embrace your mind.

la instantánea No°11

**The best Aphrodisiac
for a clever woman
is a brilliant Man.**

la instantánea No°3

**Although
I can not smell you
you so deeply ignite my senses.**

MARVELS

Just when
my belief seems running
out of date
you stumble on my doorstep
to give my stars
a new debate.
The world spins
between a glimmering aurora
letting my love cells shiver
'cause beauty
lies in trees
in hope
in
colors of the sky.

Some
newborn dreams with every step
draw a near penumbral lunar eclipse
trying to chase
this perfect perpetual smile of mine,
I guess
I have to keep on dreaming.

Have you ever thought
of the beginning
minus the end,
have you
ever thought
of the deep-seated differences
that are really
just dear marvels,
they outshine with ease
those illuminated city lights
mirrored
in my backyard window.

FIRE UNDER ICE

We met each other that evening
over some old-fashioned wooden dinner table.
Two single-minded
lonely travelers of hearts
in smoky air
as I would have found
still without a face
a Rose in winter.

Reaching out eagerly
you talked to me
with hungry eyes.

Unexpected, out of nowhere
emerges your desire,
with insatiable hunger
that lusted
for perfumed sweaty adventures.

You know the meaning of "Secrecy"
know your way with words,
after all – you were an author
to ease and calm my senses
you were telling me sweet stories
of a shell seeker's day,
a man in search of hidden treasures.

Proudly
you showed me
those gentle modest findings
soft-colored seashells,
fragile homes of the Ocean.

Meanwhile
the supposed poet
searched deeply inside
her own purse of poetry
only to find
that the words have fallen out.
There is nothing
but humiliating emptiness
and melancholic virtues.

Perhaps
it would be fun
to sail along such delicate matters,
cascades of unexplored salty erotic madness
perhaps I should taste
and allow myself to be discovered
all over once more.
We could challenge some infinite rebellious infernos
or to wave with happy rocks in our hands...

Yet I am not the one to rock the boat
seeking refuge with my heart in stubborn resistance
hiding in remote tenderness
my heart remains on fire
on fire under ice.

PINK TIGRESS

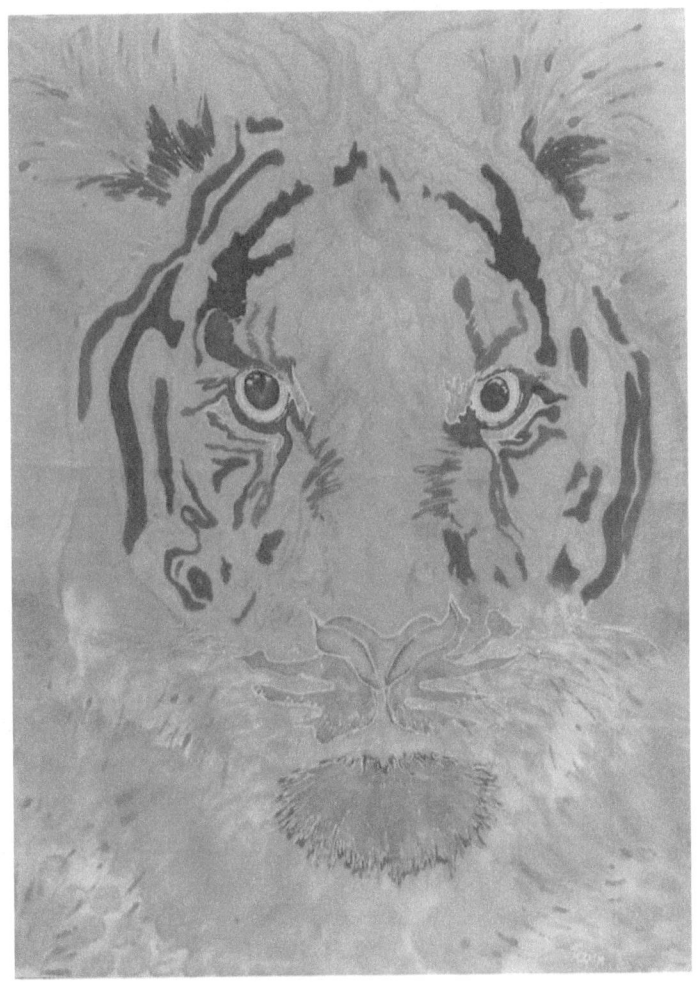

For the tigress within me. #Stefaniasilkarts

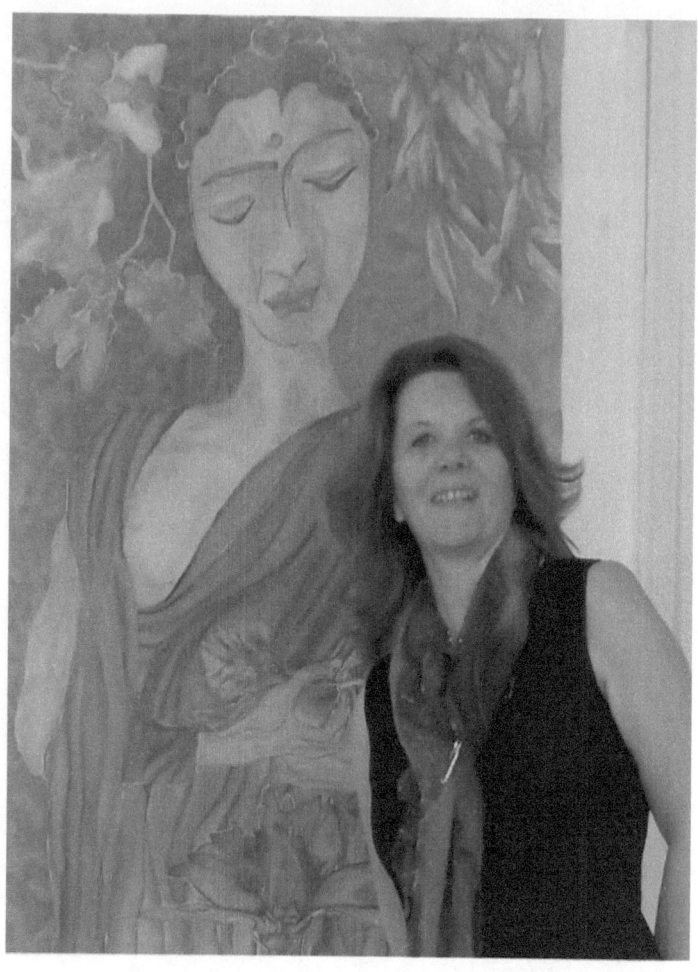

Myself and the first Buddha that I painted on Silk Satin 12.0 in Vienna 2015. I hope that I can still create many more in my lifetime.

More Info on Xokonoschtletl Gómora

I am grateful for the the enlightening connection to Xokonoschtletl.

He is a devoted and fine human being, his lives mission is dedicated to one great course: The return of the sacred Feathercrown from the 9th Montezuma Ruler which is in Exile, held in Austria at the World Museum. for the last 500 Years.

It is his lives purpose and mission not only to return thee holy Feathercrown, but to give back freedom, grace and ancient wisdom to the Mexican People.

We have created an association to help with this purpose, and Mexican/Austrian Friendship in mind, **further to save and protect rainforest from Aztek and Mayan origin in Tabasco, Mexico which is the home of Xokonoschtletl.**

For this moment in time, it is his greatest wish that with commen efforts, we can save a small dedicated Area of 8 HA together, saving space, wildlife and holy grounds before it is burned down for use with cattle.
On our website sonnengold and also, the wixsite we can offer more Info to this matter.

So far, Xokonoschtletl has spend 40 Years+ for this endeavour. He has spoken to many high profile people, including the holyness Dalai Lama,

You will find information on his profile as Author, Aztek Dancer/Drummer, UN-speaker and certified Tourist Guide for all of Mexico here:

https://sonnengold-orosolar.odoo.com

https://xokonoschtletl.wixsite.com/urwald-retten

http://www.xoko.info/

And in his own words:
My name is Xokonoschtletl Gomora.

I was born in Mexico on February 17, 1951. Since 1986, I have been coming to Europe regularly and traveling around the world to achieve a single goal: To bring back to Mexico the sacred feather crown of our Lord Montezuma, which has been in the Vienna Ethnographic Museum since 1524. This crown is of the highest spiritual and idealistic importance for the Mexican natives! This sacred crown is intended to help the peoples of Mexico preserve their own culture and identity. This was proclaimed in a message from the Council of Elders on August 12, 1521. On the following day, August 13, 1521, the last ruler of the Aztecs, KUAUHTEMOK, opened the gates of the Aztec capital, MEXICO-TENOCHTITLAN, after 93 days of siege by the Spanish.

This is my life's work. I am an organic farmer, book author, traditional Aztec dancer and certified tourist guide for the whole of Mexico. I have a great deal of knowledge about my country, traditions, cultures, rites and customs. For this job, which I have been doing for many years, I have learned German, English and Italian. In the meantime, I have given over 5000 lectures worldwide, through which I advocate peace, ecology, environmental awareness, healthy nutrition, preservation of cultures and, in particular, that we should return to nature. In these many years, I have traveled 2 million kilometers around the world, have officially addressed the United Nations seven times and have been present 17 times. I have also been received several times by the Royal Family of the Netherlands, the Pope in the Vatican, the Head of Government of Liechtenstein, three Ministers of Culture of Austria, many ambassadors, the mayors of Berlin, Amsterdam, Rome, Oslo, etc.

Since 1986, I have taken turns bringing 440 indigenous people from Mexico to Europe to support me in this task. Everything I have done so far I have had to finance myself: through the sale of my books, the production of traditional handicrafts, through my lectures, seminars and workshops as well as the trips I have organized to Mexico.

I am also chairman of an international cultural association for international understanding, whose headquarters are in Mexico, with sister associations in Austria, Switzerland, Germany, Belgium and Denmark. I spend several months a year in Europe because of my fight for the feather crown. I have a lot of strength.... but I also need a lot of support, especially financially... because the costs of this fight are enormous!

My greatest wish is to return home with the Holy Crown as soon as possible - to my beloved motherland ANAHUAK!!!

Thank you for your interest,

Stefanie Wilhelm & Xokonoschtletl
Verein Sonnengold-Orosolar Wien

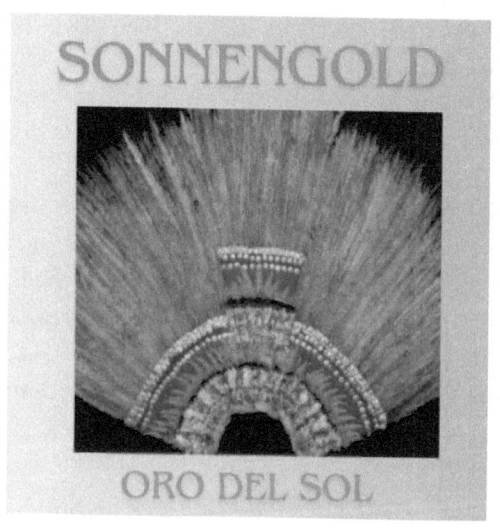

Acknowledgments

My gratitude is with all the lovely humans that have supported, inspired, encouraged or even criticized me in my ongoing artistic thriving way.
We are all here to learn, to be happy and grateful.

It is that I am only feeling sincerely alive since I have embraced that fact that I am an Artist, this was a development and took its own time in my awareness. These poems that I wrote were born particular in the last twenty or-so-more-years, in which I have overcome a serious Stage III Breast cancer.
Ten years later, I accompanied my close Mexican friend in his process of long illness and was with him in his last moments of life due to heart troubles and brain bleeding. It was my chance to gain so much understanding about life, the natural progress of death and dying, beside its acceptance as it being part of our life. Having done so well, it seems almost cynical to find out that once more I have to fight for my life again.
My heart has taken massive damage from those chemical drugs. More than twenty years later, it manifested itself in my heart muscle. Weakening it by 70 percent.

So, once again I dance a Waltz with the Devil and while his sand clock is still swinging; I might as well sing a Song! Death is no longer this mysterious, dark frightening energy to me. I have learned that it also can even be our friend, more so, I feel it is nothing more than a gate that we walk through, similar to a cellular barrier.

Something we have to master at the end of our life, the crowning of a kind, and we better meet him gracefully with an open heart and mind. I have been visited more than once from friends (or souls) of "the other side", always in energetical ways.

Let me assure you: It is a beautiful encounter.

I have received help, spiritual advice or simply love, joy and strength. Never was I in danger of any kind.

So, when I asked myself "The big why" I came to the solution, that if I am to meet such themes of illness, it must be to encounter my own inner healing abilities, to embrace self-love and to overcome fear of any kind that is hidden within myself.

This is an ongoing process of learning. In this same way I work with my artistic abilities and creative resources, both in painting and writing. Along the way, while traveling and of course, also via social media, I have met many beautiful people. They all have left a mark and to my great joy, many I even know personally.

In particular I wish to thank the following special friends:

Mahmud Mahmudzade, Baku/Azerbaijan and TX/U.S.A
For his wonderful art, deep in color and emotion.
He is an intense soul filled with secret wisdom.
I adore him as a long-term friend, painter, photographer and architect. Mahmud is the most poetic painter that I know of. More than once has he been the source to my poetry. More than once has he supported me in my simple ways.

Daniel Jean-Baptiste, Can/St. Lucia for his charming and folly
ways in which he took me "by the hand" as mentor, friend, artistic advisor and more than anything, leading international silk artist.
His silk art is energetical and magical too, always with that great Caribbean touch shining brightly on silk. He has a generous heart, it is impossible not to love him. I am always grateful for his connection, most certainly Daniel holds a special place in my heart.

Martina Scheinost, Bamberg/Germany.
I love Martina's hands-on

no-drama approach to life. She has supported me in both physical and financial ways and is never far away if I need a friend for either advise or a simple smile. If ever you are stuck in Bamberg (Bavaria) and need a place to stay, she will be able to help you. Needless to say, she is a like-minded silk painter.

Angelika Gregoric ("Angel") Vienna/Austria.
Fashion Designer, Yoga Expert, Traveler – I am so blessed to call Angel my dear friend.
She has an open heart for every occasion, and is particularly fond of a "certain Kangaroo", (by Marc Uwe Kling). With her huge energy, she left nothing short to turn me into a common fan as well.
Angel would sign blindly the order to go for your dreams, which is why she captured my heart too, of course.

Francisco Quesada de Huete, San José, CR, Oil on canvas
with whom I shared cozy talks, lovely stories and great discussions about art and life in his studio while visiting his beautiful amazing country, Costa Rica. His pointed Art on large canvasses is unmistakable in great "Tico" style:
Tender, powerful Landscapes rich in color and composition.

Jeannina Blanco Fine Arts, San José, CR.
When thinking of Jeannina, I
see a huge warm smile. A true Entrepreneur, she is smart
and lovely. We shared ideas for business and greatly fired
each other on. Thanks to her I could offer silk painting
workshops in her studio. Jeannina loves to paint in oil.
Exceptional Portraits as well as open Street scenes or
famous buildings, always with that special female focus
in both classical and modern style. It makes me happy,
to know her as my friend.

Baisakhi Saha, San José, CR. Author, Dancer
It is difficult, to point down a residence for my dear
Indian friend Baisakhi, which I met on a Mexican
Festival in San José. She has traveled to over twenty
Countries, speaks more than eight languages, is TedX
Speaker, Author, and loves to dance. Above all, Bai is an
amazing woman and proud human being. She allows
herself to follow her heart and spiritual development,
which she shares on social media and through her books.
In doing so, she inspires others, encouraging personal
growth. I am glad, she is a terrible cook, how else can
you endure so much greatness? Indeed, I am awfully
fond and proud of her.

Nicky Spaulding Arts, Miami/Fl. Entrepreneur / Artist

Luckily, I had the exceptional chance to meet Nicky in his Studio while he offered me "a tour", telling me mesmerizing stories of his art. His warmth, humor and brilliance is one of a kind. Nicky is fun and made this brief afternoon a highlight, which sparkles long into my life. When I see his bold art, my heart starts to fly and I can start writing poetry, too.

The Poet I love most, which gave me bread, fire and water was the unforgettable Chilean *Pablo Neruda*. I owe him much.

There were others too, that helped me to carry myself over troubled waters, one of which is American Poet *Elizabeth Bishop*. I was fascinated by both her poetry and lifestyle, and the unforeseeable turns it took. In particular with her Brazilian Partner, the adorable Architect, Lota de Macedo Soares, who so tragically later took her life. Bishop instead had a hunger for life, and was intellectually ambitious. Women like that inspire me, I take them as role models more over they offer me revelation.

It is with much love and honor that I wish to remember certain days of despair and struggle with Francisco, particular in his last months, when he was so obviously ill and needed care. Two people were a beacon of ight and hope. The provided us with fun along with lightness, something I will always be grateful for:

Thank you, *Susanne & Frank Welsch-Lehmann*, Kronberg for your outstanding support one whole year when probably I needed help the most. You are so special.

And finally, also the Russian Cellist, Prof. *Viktor Miloserdov*/Vienna.
A classical Solo-Cellist, who plays his beloved Violoncello with nothing less than devotion and a constant thrive for excellence. He believes in self-development above all, expression of freedom in spirit and mind. I learned much from you, even about myself, I feel obliged for all you gave me. You were my hardest teacher but we can be proud above all to stay friends that help each other in difficult times.
I am deeply grateful that so beautiful human beings touched my life, thus enriching mine so much! My poetry is reflecting images of each chapter, of which you are part in days of rain and sunshine. Thank you and with much love.

MAY YOU ALL BE SAVE, HEALTHY AND HAPPY!
STEFANIE WILHELM, #STEFANIASILKARTS

la instantanea No°11

It so happens

from time to time

that one must fly

off into the winds.

la Instantánea No°6

In the eye of beauty
everything becomes art.

www.ingramcontent.com/pod-product-compliance
Lightning Source LLC
Chambersburg PA
CBHW020605220526
45463CB00006B/2464